John Elia

SHARE & SPREAD
His Word!

Ken Byrne

SAVED!!!
What it means to me

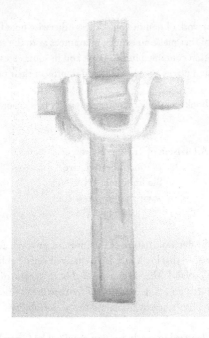

Personal stories from "born-again" Christians, about
their individual lives, salvation, and the change since
they accepted Jesus Christ.

KEN BYRNE

WESTBOW
PRESS®
A DIVISION OF THOMAS NELSON
& ZONDERVAN

WestBow Press books may be ordered through booksellers or by contacting:

WestBow Press
A Division of Thomas Nelson & Zondervan
1663 Liberty Drive
Bloomington, IN 47403
www.westbowpress.com
844-714-3454

ISBN: 978-1-6642-1342-5 (sc)
ISBN: 978-1-6642-1343-2 (e)

Library of Congress Control Number: 2020923101

Print information available on the last page.

WestBow Press rev. date: 11/24/2020

Contents

Foreword

Some thoughts before you read these stories from people who have experienced the transformation of just living in this world to becoming a different person devoted to the Living God, Jesus Christ.

After I was saved and became a believer, a born-again Christian, my world changed for the better. A couple of years ago, I woke up one morning with one thing on my mind; to try and reach as many people, as possible, with my testimony of salvation.

After thinking about it, I decided to include the stories of other people and share their testimonies.

I sometimes ask people from church, and friends, when they came to **know** and accept Jesus as their Saviour. Very emotional to hear a person talk about their life stories and the things they went through and then, finally, surrender to God completely.

Somehow, I really think that the Holy Spirit has asked me to write this book to reach people that are curious about "born-again" Christians or followers of Jesus Christ.

Perhaps you will relate to someone's story and realize how they overcame the trials in their life and then know that no one is in a hopeless situation when you have Jesus Christ waiting to pick you up.

I thought I was in a desperate health situation twelve years ago when even trying to hold the weight of a pencil was difficult. Here I am now typing away trying to reach you and as many people as possible.

Did you ever think to yourself that I am too sinful to be forgiven? Just about everyone on planet Earth has heard the song, "Amazing Grace" that was written by John Newton, an ex-slave trader.

You should Google this man and read his story. Believe me when I say that no person is beyond the acceptance of Jesus Christ.

Enjoy these real-life stories.…

Ken

Acknowledgments

The seed was planted in my brain to write this book when I had a dream one night. When I woke in the morning, this whole project of telling people's testimonies of salvation and their personal stories was heavy on my mind. So, I would be remiss not to mention what I feel is my driving force - God, the Holy Spirit. I really feel that a connection to someone's story in this book will demonstrate that we are not hopeless in God's eyes.

To my wife, Jane, I thank you for being that person who introduced me to God's Word, the Bible. Being the editor for this book is appreciated and your patience is admired.

To Kristin Stockton, the young and incredibly talented member of our church who designed the cover artwork. The thought you put into this drawing is amazing.

To each contributor, your individual testimony of your life and salvation is so appreciated. This is a discipleship opportunity by opening up and explaining how God's love changed your life. To share your life experiences and how you came to know and accept Jesus is a blessing in itself.

To Pastor Rick Dobrowolski thank you for your insight and developing a salvation plan. Hopefully, this will open someone's mind and, more importantly, someone's heart to the Word of God (the Bible).

The scripture verses in this book were quoted from the Word of God. The reference Bible that I used is titled "The Lucado *Life Lessons Study Bible*" and it is the New King James Version (NKJV). Scripture taken from the New King James Version. Copyright 1982 by Thomas Nelson, Inc. Used by permissions. All rights reserved.

My personal inscription on the inside cover, of my Bible, a quotation from John Bunyan: "Sin will keep you from this book or this book will keep you from sin!"

Ken Byrne's personal story

When someone tells me the story of his or her salvation, it fascinates me. Every person's story is different than the other.

What's intriguing about a person's life story? It encompasses the time **before they got saved, the day of their salvation** and, **the impact since then**.

I was born in 1947 to Catholic parents, George, and Beatrice, and went to a Roman Catholic church and school in Syracuse, New York. I was always curious about the "teachings of the religion", and I had many questions but was met with the response, "These are things you don't question". Yes, I had plenty of questions but no answers. I wanted to know more about Adam and Eve. Who was it that witnessed these events and recorded them? It was a simple thing for a ten-year-old to ask, but I did not find out the answer for another fifty-five years! I went to the Catholic Mass almost every Sunday and was an altar boy while growing up. I was not the most attentive student and well-behaved was not in my vocabulary; maybe that is why the nuns and priests called me Dennis the Menace.

In 1964, I quit high school after my junior year and joined the U.S. Navy for a four-year enlistment. There I received my high school GED and worked in radar electronics.

Our ship had a multitude of different types of religious services, and out of curiosity, I attended each and every one of them to see the difference. I was totally confused now!

Finally, my four-year navy service was complete and I was back in civilian life. I eventually joined a Roman Catholic men's organization, Knights of Columbus. My highest position obtained was Deputy Grand Knight, fourth degree for the district of South Yarmouth, Massachusetts. I was dubbed "Sir Kenneth" in the organization.

By the year 2007, I had *two* failed marriages behind me and was now living with a woman out of wedlock. While in Massachusetts, I owned a real estate business on Cape Cod and lived in comfort - money, luxury cars, frequent trips to the casino, and great vacations. I thought I had it all (or did I?).

Then at the age of fifty-nine, my world started falling apart. While driving home from a family reunion in Syracuse, New York, I started getting double vision. Within weeks, I developed muscle weakness and sensitivity to light both outside in the sun and inside the house. Long story short: myasthenia gravis, a neurological disorder, was my enemy.

A year and a half later, the weakness increased and breathing was becoming tough. I was admitted into a Boston hospital and then told that my lungs were filling up with fluid, which the medical staff started draining. I could hardly blow a feather from the palm of my hand.

One night the doctor decided last rites would be in order, so a Catholic priest was summoned. He went through his motions of absolving my sins and preparing me for heaven. Well, the next morning, I was still alive and was lying in the hospital bed with one thing on my mind: **IF** my *sins* were forgiven the night before **THEN,** why didn't I feel relieved or cleansed? Little did I know it would take another five years for me to get an answer for that! So, the doctors operated and removed my thymus and started me on heavy duty meds and therapy.

For the next year, or so, I lost everything, my real estate business, money, and friends. My weakness was so extreme that just holding a pencil was difficult. Walking was almost impossible without some kind of assistance. It took all the strength I could muster just to put my socks on in the morning. Finally, I came to the point that I could take care of myself. Then I packed my things and moved from Cape Cod to Pennsylvania to be closer to my daughter Amy, her husband and my three grandchildren.

Amy recommended that I check out an "over

sixty-two" community. I applied for an apartment and when it came time to process my application, I sat in the lobby waiting for the staff person to go over my information.

The admissions coordinator, Jane, was extremely helpful. I will never forget her since she was the one to change my life forever. My first impression of her was a beautiful woman who was organized and pleasant, with a no-nonsense demeanor (and those eyes). I could appreciate that, I thought.

Eventually, I moved into a newly constructed senior housing building, and it was only a five-minute drive to Jane's office. My interaction with Jane was frequent because I was elected the president of the resident association. After a while, I discovered Jane was a widow, and there I was, hmmm… a single man (again)! Actually, neither one of us was looking to develop a relationship with each other or anyone else. We kept everything on a business level.

However, I probably spent an ample amount of time in her office, because Jane was trying to distance herself from me. The many "professional" meetings were taking longer and maybe getting too personal. She thought perhaps talking about God might be a deterrent. Well, that **backfired**! I was a frustrated Catholic man with so many questions.

The more she spoke about God, the more questions I had, and I continued coming to see her.

She gave me a DVD titled "Why Did Jesus Have to Die?", and I watched it, and enjoyed listening to the preacher, who spoke all about salvation. Then Jane decided this was too important to ignore. Was God using Jane?

My sixty-fifth birthday was fast approaching, and she decided to give me a present: "The Lucado Life Lessons Study Bible", NKJV. Jane had a note enclosed suggesting some reading for me. The books of Romans and John were a good start. I, of course, would have started on page one of Genesis. That is what people usually do, right? They start at the beginning of a book. Then she wrote out a plan of salvation for me. The last sentence of Jane's note kept needling me, "**What are you waiting for?**".

Because I had so many questions for most of my life, this was an opportunity I did not want to pass up. The timing could not have been better. Seventeen days after I received the Bible and plan of salvation, I felt compelled to confess my sins.

I read that even though sin has damaged my relationship with God, the Father, JESUS CHRIST can fix it!!!

So, on June 6, 2012, I went into my bedroom at 9:00 p.m. and knelt at the foot of my bed. With my Bible in front of me, I placed my forehead on top of it, I confessed my sins (as much as I could remember). I asked for forgiveness and for Jesus Christ to be my Lord and Savior.

I prayed to God all the time growing up, probably because I wanted something that would benefit me. My prayers were different now, I decided to just talk to Jesus like I never had before. Now I realized that God knew me even before I was born. He knew everything I had ever thought, said, or done!

Still, I felt I needed to mention as many of my wrongdoings (sins) as I could recall. I had been searching my mind from childhood and forward for the past couple of days. I asked for His forgiveness and for His help to give me the strength not to sin anymore. So, I prayed,

"Almighty Father, You sent your Son, Jesus, from heaven to our sinful earth… to take on human form as a baby from Mary, a virgin not of royalty but from a simple family. You sent Him to become an adult, to choose twelve apostles, and to teach and spread Your Word.

I believe that Jesus was tortured, suffered, and nailed to a cross. He died on that tree and shed His blood for our sins so we may have the chance of salvation… an eternity with You in heaven. *This I believe!*"

As I knelt there the tears flowed down my face. I finally felt cleansed for the first time! I thought, *I am saved!*

People of many religions consider themselves

Christians, but I would like to be known as a believer or a follower of Jesus Christ. I just entered into a relationship with Jesus Christ.

"For God so loved the world that He gave His only begotton son, that whoever believes in Him should not perish but have everlasting life." (John 3:16 NKJV)

Since my salvation, my attitude has changed so much. I am not judgmental toward anyone. I still slip up during stressful times, and that may never change, but with the guidance of the Holy Spirit, I will, over time, think before acting, speaking, or going through any difficult thought processes.

There is an inner peace knowing that on judgment day, Jesus will take my hand and lead me into the Promised Land... for eternity.

SIX months after I got saved, Jane and I became husband and wife. The wedding was a family affair. Jane's three adult children had essential roles. Rick, Jane's son and Head Pastor of Allentown Bible Church, officiated.

Rachel, Jane's daughter, was matron-of-honor and the piano player. That left Peter, Jane's son, to walk his mom down the aisle and give her to me! My daughter, Amy, was the bridesmaid. My brother Mike honored me as my best man.

My sister Ginny flew in from Kansas, and we had a couple of special days together before the wedding day. She even thought it was a riot that I wore a kilt to the rehearsal, and I definitely think the grandkids were confused by that! They were asking, "Why is Grandpa wearing a skirt?"

The wedding was on December 15th, and the weather was perfect for that time of the year, sunny with the temperature in the seventies.

About a year later, we moved into a townhouse in Quakertown and became members at the Allentown Bible Church. These members had heard pleas, from Jane, to pray for my salvation. The Bible does explain the importance of church and fellowship.

At church, one thing really stood out to me, something I had not seen before in a church; everyone had a Bible opened to the place where Pastor Rick was preaching. I felt these members were now my brothers and sisters and took a genuine interest in me, and without judging.

My personal life changed. I do not gossip. The swearing was reduced to hardly ever. If I happened to slip because of an aggressive driver, or whatever, I immediately felt deep quilt and again asked for forgiveness. I do know that when I was saved it was from all my sins... the past, present and future. It's the new attitude, walk and being a follower of Jesus that makes the difference.

I also have a deep concern about other people and what they are going through. I participate in prayer requests; if someone is going through a difficult time and ask me to pray for them, I immediately say "sure", take their hand and pray. Doing that makes it sincere for them and shows how easy it is to talk with God. Not a formal prayer but a conversation with God, putting your troubles at His feet to sort out. He has a plan for each and every one of us.

I knew someone, aged in his fifties, who had a reading challenge and found it almost impossible to read his Bible. He lived nearby, so I offered Bible reading at our home.

After a couple of months of weekly sessions, he opened up by telling me Heaven was vital because he wanted to be with his parents. I explained the plan of salvation to him. Weeks went by, and he felt 75% saved now! Had to break it to him, you must submit yourself to the Lord completely. You cannot be 50 or 75% saved, salvation is surrendering and accepting Jesus Christ completely.

More time passed by with weekly meetings, and he had plenty of questions. He had a thirst to know more about Jesus, excited to learn and he was soaking up the words of the Bible like a dry sponge reacting to water.

One Sunday driving to church, a 30-minute ride with our friend, he wanted to know more about salvation. He wanted to be saved but still didn't know how. Everyone will talk to God on their own behalf knowing they are submitting to Him and accepting Him as their Lord and Saviour. Well, we immediately pulled into a parking lot and guided him.

It did not take long for our friend to admit that he was a sinner, to ask God to forgive him and ask Him to be his Lord and Savior. Our friend was **saved**, and tears flowed down his face. He was now totally submitted to the Lord. At church, he told others all about his salvation and how thrilled he felt.

I have been thinking about the stories people have shared with me in the past few years, always being fascinated to hear about their lives and eventual salvation. If only I could reach out to explain this to others – it would be such a blessing. Hopefully, they would open their hearts and minds to ask questions, to get answers and to accept Jesus Christ as their Savior, as I did. So, here I am, feeling that my discipleship mission is to write this book.

And, by the way, I did finally find out who wrote the book of Genesis. Moses received the information for the first five books of the Bible, directly from God, while on Mt. Sinai. The Bible, authored by God, is amazing. Do not wait 65 years, like I did, to read it. *What are you waiting for?*

NKJV John 3: 16, 17

16. For God so loved the world that he gave his only Son, that whoever believes in him should not perish but have eternal life.

17. For God did not send his Son into the world to condemn the world, but in order that the world might be saved through him.

Jane A. Byrne's
personal story

I was born in Poland and lived on a farm in a beautiful village. My family, and the whole village, was Roman Catholic, and we attended church on a regular basis. The priests in that church knew the families well and were recognized by all the villagers.

I enjoyed the different traditions in the church, especially during the holidays. Easter traditions were my favorite. I also liked to ask the priests questions. By the time I was eleven, I had decided that I wanted to be a nun and kept on thinking and talking about it for the next two years. I was discouraged out of it after I arrived in the U.S.A.

My father, sister, and I came to the United States (not knowing any English) in April of 1963. I was twelve then. My mother stayed in Poland – a long story as to why. She and my baby brother, Stanley, joined us a year later. For the rest of that school year, my sister and I lived with my aunt and uncle in Lansdale while our father worked and lived in Philadelphia.

While driving around with them, we would pass by different churches. In Poland, I only saw Catholic Churches. But here, in the United States, there are many different kinds of churches and my aunt was patiently explaining the differences between them and then finally gave up.

While passing by a Baptist church in Lansdale, Pennsylvania, she bluntly told me to stop asking questions about it because I will *not ever* step in there anyway.

At the end of August we moved in with my father and in May of 1964 our mother and brother arrived from Poland. By then, I questioned a lot of things in the Catholic Church. I tried my best to follow the rules and regulations but felt that there had to be more. I wanted to be closer to God but did not know how to achieve that.

By the time I was a senior in high school, I would talk to God - not just saying the regular prayers prescribed by the Catholic Church - but really talk to Him. He would answer some of those prayers in a way that would really make me think! One of the answers to my prayers still is very fresh in my mind.

Before I had to go for my orientation at a college, I found out that they had no dorms on their campus. This was going to be a problem since I did not have a car. I had to find a place to live. Two of my classmates, who already had their orientations, told me that they were not able to find a place close to the campus.

When I met with the college counselor, he gave me a list of people that housed students and advised that I look at those places that are farther away because those closest to the campus were surely filled by now.

When I left his office, I had a strong feeling that I should first look at the closest ones. The first home was only a block and a half away. No one was at home. As I was going back to the car (a family friend drove me there and was waiting in the car), a lady from across the street waved to me and told me that they were away and did not have any more room for students. Then she asked me to cross over and talk to her.

Today everything from my past makes sense, but at that time, I did not know the amazing way God answers prayers. Let me explain. This lady told me later that she rarely went to the front of her house. Something drew her there that day. She wanted to house two college girls but did not have time to redo the second bedroom. When she saw me, she liked how I looked, smiled, and talked to her and decided right then and there to show me the other bedroom. It had beautiful old furniture and a blooming apple tree just outside the window! I liked it immediately. I took the room and loved living in that house with her and another girl from the campus, and it was such a short walk to the campus! Thank you, Lord!

I believe that God was working in my life from when I was a young girl, even when I still lived in that small Polish village and attended a Catholic Church.

I wanted to know Him better, and He was giving me the opportunities. My neighbors, where I lived when attending college the first two years, were Christians. They took me to their church a few times where I heard the gospel, but I did not respond then.

The first year Walt and I were married, we went to a farmer's market located nearby. In one section there were tables with lots of books for sale. I love to read, so I picked out quite a few.

There were also some Bibles and my husband, made a remark that maybe I should read something more worthwhile. He picked one up and placed it on top of the books I already had in my arms. We bought it and when we arrived home, I started reading it.

The more I read the Bible, the more questions I had to ask the priests. I spoke to a priest in my parish in Philadelphia. He answered some of my questions but could not clearly explain the verse "Jesus answered and said to him, most assuredly, I say to you, unless one is born of water and the Spirit, he cannot enter the kingdom of God." (NKJV John 3:5).

The priest was not happy with me reading the Bible and told me so! To make matters worse, he told my parents about all this, and they were not pleased with me either. Not happy about me reading the Bible??

Then came a Friday, sometime in the middle of May, in 1976. It started just like any typical day. I went to work in the morning and then planned to spend a quiet evening at home, reading. Walt, who worked for a finance company at that time, usually worked late on Fridays. But, as soon as I got home, I received a phone call from my cousin Lorraine. She was the daughter of the aunt that my sister and I lived with when we first arrived in the U.S.A.

Lorraine was a few years older than me, and we did not keep in touch much, mainly because I lived in Philadelphia. Lorraine had attended the evangelistic meetings, which were held at her church this whole week. On Wednesday evening, the evangelist asked if they would bring someone, who was not saved yet, to the Friday evening service. Lorraine was one of those who raised her hand to indicate that she will do her best to bring someone. She asked everyone she could think of, but no one would come with her.

Then she took out her personal address book and, starting at the beginning, called everyone she had not yet talked to.

When she came to my name and, remembering that I just moved to Lansdale, called me. She asked me if I would like to go with her to a revival meeting this evening. I had no idea what a revival meeting was, but wanted to reconnect with Lorraine again, so I decided to go.

So that is how I ended up in the Baptist Church in Lansdale, PA., the same church that Lorraine's mother, my aunt, claimed I would never step foot in. After we sat down I looked around and saw that there were no statues, stained glass windows, or a crucifix of Jesus on an altar (or even an altar!). I knew we were in some kind of church, but it looked more like an auditorium and much different from the Catholic churches I had been in all my life.

I asked Lorraine about the place. She told me that we were at a church and explained it all to me. She even said to me that she was sorry for not explaining what a revival meeting was and not making it more precise as to where it was going to be. She told me that she did not mean to deceive me in any way.

Oh well, I told myself, no big deal and told her not to worry about it. Then we stood up to sing. Wow!!! Everyone was singing! It was so beautiful I had goose bumps on my arms. It has been a long time (back when I was in Poland) since I heard people sing so well in church.

A couple more songs and a few words from the pastor and then the evangelist came to the podium. I received another shock. The many questions I was asking the Catholic priests? Well, this evangelist was answering them one by one! He had my full attention. At the end of his sermon, he started asking us questions.

"Do we want to get closer to God? Do we want

Jesus to be our Savior?" I remember thinking "of course, who would not want that?"

I raised my hand when he asked for a show of hands. When he looked in my direction and asked if I meant it, I nodded my head and lowered my hand again. Then came the invitation to go forward to the church's front if we want to accept Jesus as our Savior. Well, that was another matter. I was so nervous I could not move. Lorraine must have noticed me raising my hand because she told me that she would accompany me if I wanted to go. I nodded, but still could not move! We sang a song right before that invitation and I was still holding onto my songbook. She had to pull it out of my hand. Then we went to the front together. I had no idea what was going to happen when we got there. A lady with a Bible came up to us. She took me to one of the small rooms behind the front of the church where we talked.

Lorraine stayed in the central part of the church. The lady showed me, from the Bible, how to receive Jesus as my Lord and Savior, and I gladly did that. When we came back into the church and I told Lorraine what happened, she was almost in tears and gave me a big hug.

When I got home, my husband was already in bed and wanted to know where I was so late. I tried to tell him about it but he told me that he wanted to go to sleep because he had to leave at five in the morning for his two-week army reserve training. My story would have to wait until he returned.

Well, I went with Lorraine to both Sunday services and Wednesday prayer meetings for the two weeks he was away. She also met with me once a week for a follow-up Bible study. By the time Walt returned home I was fully committed to attending the Baptist church.

When Walt came home from training, I explained everything, He was not thrilled, and neither were my parents when they heard about it. They were so upset with me for not attending the Catholic Church anymore that they did not even want to bother with me and for quite a long time. But after Rachel, and then Rick, were born, they had to see more of me in order to visit with their only grandchildren. (Peter was not born yet.)

I lost friends, and some of my relatives distanced themselves from me. Some only because they felt I hurt my parents. But I was not going to turn back.

To learn the Bible better, I took a four-year program in a Bible Institute, which was provided to church members and taught mostly by the church's leadership team and seminary professors.

Meanwhile, there was a lot of fear, trouble, pain, and frustration to deal with at home. When Rachel was four and Rick almost three years old, something happened between my husband and me that I had a tough time dealing with. After putting the children down for a nap, I went to my room, closed the door, and completely broke down. I was hurting so much that I just wanted to die.

I remember begging God to do something because I could not go on like this anymore. I asked Him to either take control of it all or take me home. I don't know how long I stayed like this. I was kneeling by the side of my bed with my face pressed against the covers so the children would not hear me cry. Then I started to feel like someone was in the room with me. That feeling was so strong that I picked up my head and looked around. I could not see anyone, but it still felt like someone was there.

While I was contemplating all this, I suddenly realized a change coming over me. I felt a deep peace and then strength.

Did I get saved at this time, was I finally and totally surrendered to the Lord?

That was a question I would ask myself often in the next few weeks. Did anything in my life change after that? No! The difference from then on was that **I** started to change. I had more peace and started depending more on God. I smiled more and started to get involved in the church more.

But that big question kept on bothering me because _if I was not saved in 1976 then how valid was my baptism?_ I got baptized in July of the same year.

Then I finally started praying about this. My church pastor started preaching about baptism at the Wednesday evening services. Talk about timing. I began to get convicted and decided to get baptized again. I talked to another pastor, and he advised me to do that and do it as soon as possible so I would not have to think about it anymore. There was a scheduled baptism set in two weeks.

It was also the evening of the Christmas Cantata, a special Christmas presentation by our choir and orchestra. What an evening that was!

Walt invited a friend of his to come to the Christmas Cantata this year and to have dinner with us beforehand. We ended up with a single man, having dinner with Rachel, Rick, and me that evening – with my husband being away! Walt knew his friend was coming over, but he thought his girlfriend was coming with him too. Walt's friend did not know Walt was going to be away and did not bother to call to let us know that his girlfriend was not accompanying him. During dinner, I told him that I would be getting baptized before the program at the church. He asked a lot of questions about salvation and baptism. That's almost all we talked about till it was time to leave.

The church was packed. There were two of us to be baptized that evening, but the other person backed out for some reason.

I was so nervous I do not even remember what I said just before they put me in the water. Right before the baptism the person being baptized tells everyone their testimony of how they accepted Christ as their Savior.

A couple of weeks later that friend of Walt's called.

He wanted me to be the first one to know that he also accepted Christ as his Savior!

When Peter was a month-old, Rick (at age five) was baptized and joined the church. Walt rededicated his life and joined the church (he had been dropped from membership a while back). I was so sure that everything now will get better. But, in just a few months, Walt started attending church less and less, and things at home were getting pretty bad again.

Then in 1998, Walt decided he did not want to work for anyone anymore. All he wanted to do was buy things and sell them at flea markets. He was not able to make much money doing that, and we finally agreed that I should get a full-time job.

At this time, I was homeschooling Peter, cleaned two houses (I was able to take him with me so he would do his schoolwork there), and substituting at the Baptist school, where I could also take Peter with me. Before I even applied anywhere I prayed and wrote down what I would like in a job and then prayed again before going to interviews.

Well, I was hired and started working for a senior housing community (for over 62 years old) in February of 1999. This company's position met most of the things on my job wish list.

Meanwhile, Walt's health was getting worse, and he died in February 2010. A week later, I found out that our house was in foreclosure, and my car was going to be repossessed.

I can say without a doubt that I made it through the next two years because God helped me, protected me, and provided for me, by using my children, coworkers, relatives, and friends.

My parents, who lived with Walt and me for three years by then, went to live at a continuous care facility and I moved in with Peter until a staff apartment became available in one of the buildings of the main campus where I worked.

I planned to live there until I would retire, but God had other plans. I became an Admissions Director for the new buildings that were constructed at a new location. It was a five-minute drive from the main campus where I was living.

One of the applicants for an apartment at the first new building was Ken Byrne. I never EVER wanted to get involved with a man again, especially one that is not even a Christian! But Ken would not give up. I had tried everything to discourage him, but nothing worked.

Finally, I decided to talk to him about the Lord almost every time I would see him. I was sure that he would get turned off by it and leave me alone. But, to my amazement, he would come to my office even more often and would also ask questions about God!

Then I decided to tell Rachel about all this. I was hoping she would give me some ideas on how I could get this man away from me. Well, the conversation did not go as I planned. Not only did she not give me such ideas, but she was irritated by my attitude! Her question really stunned me. "How do you know that God is not trying to use you to reach Ken?" she said.

Oh no! What do I do now?!

I bought a "Life Lessons Study Bible" NJKV by Max Lucado and a booklet describing each book of the Bible. Now, how do I give it to him? And what do I say? Rachel suggested that I accept his invitation to dinner or lunch and use that time to talk to him about the Lord. The only problem with that was that he finally stopped asking me out! All he did now was stop by my office (too often) to update me about the resident association matters. But then he usually found a way to talk about other things - of personal nature!

So, Rachel said, I will have to be the one to ask him to go somewhere since this conversation will need to be away from the office. Really?! I prayed and then hoped that maybe he would ask me for lunch again, and then all I will have to do is say 'ok'. Well, it did not happen. He really did stop asking!

Then I remembered that his sixty-fifth birthday would be coming soon. It's a good thing for the admissions director to ask the president of the resident association out to lunch on such a significant birthday, right?

When I finally got the courage to do it, I was so nervous my legs were shaking! It also did not help to see the amused expression on his face! He did not know the REAL reason for us going out to lunch. (To this day, he tells everyone that I asked him out on our first date!) Hmmm, men!

We were not able to talk much in the restaurant, so I suggested that we go for a ride because I needed to speak to him about something important. We talked for about two hours, and I also gave him his gifts. He loved the Bible. I asked him to read the Books of John and Romans in the New Testament first. He read them both within two weeks!

He had a lot of questions, so we talked almost every day. Then he asked if he could go to the church that I attended. Not only did he talk to me even more often but now he also wanted to go to church with me! I gave up.

I thought it would be a good idea for him to go to Allentown Bible Church. Many people there already knew about him and we were praying for him.

Three weeks after he started reading the Bible, he accepted Christ as his Lord and Savior. Just a month later he was baptized and it was the same church that I was baptized in. By then, we were good friends, and (hold onto your seatbelts) six months after I gave him the Bible, we got married.

Now I live in a beautiful home – the nicest I have ever lived in – with my second husband, Ken, who loves the Lord and me. We are close to all our children and grandchildren. And I still work and enjoy working for the same company.

Where am I spiritually, and what do I want to accomplish with the remainder of my life? I am dependent on God to help me get through each day. I have no clue where He is taking me, but I trust Him and know that wherever that may be ...

He will be there with me.

My favorite verse is:

"Trust in the Lord with all your heart and lean not on your own understanding: in all your ways acknowledge Him, and He shall direct your paths." (Proverbs 3: 5 and 6 NKJV)

NKJV Ephesians 2:8-9

8: For by grace you have been saved through faith, and that not of yourselves; *it is* the gift of God.

9: not of works, lest anyone should boast.

Howard's personal story

Some people have been turned around, stopped in their tracks, and transformed into Christians, as was Paul (also called Saul) on the road to Damascus. We read the story of Paul's experience in Bible, the NKJV version, the Book of Acts.

Paul was on his way to Damascus for evil reasons. He and several of his friends were planning to round up Christians, arrest them as common criminals and bring them to Jerusalem. Paul was a great persecutor of Christians. He had no time for them, nor understanding of them. He was present at the stoning of Stephen, the first Christian martyr. Paul, before his Damascus experience, was no friend to followers of Christ.

In a roundabout way, this is somewhat my story. I was not stoning any Christians. I was not planning any arrests. I was not hunting any criminals. But until November 1965, there was a criminal in my life!

I did not recognize it as such. I was not fully aware of its presence. You see---my criminal was my sin.

I was living a carefree life of my own, little caring for God's things and my relationship with Jesus Christ.

I had been married for eight years, and we had four children. My wife was a practicing Catholic, and I was a Protestant. Unfortunately, our marriage was not what it should have been, and in November of 1965, my wife and I broke up and put the children in foster homes. Any attempt at reconciliation was in vain. Friends and others tried to help, but nothing worked. Our marriage was doomed.

By Christmas, the child welfare agency asked me if I could take the children home for Christmas, and I told them I did not have a place to take them. They suggested I ask the Mission personnel for help.

So, I went to the Mission and told them my problem and asked for their help. They said they would let me and my children sleep there as a family for Christmas and that we could spend Christmas day there and have dinner with others at the mission.

Knowing my problem, the minister of the Mission came to me Christmas morning and talked to me about my issues and my spiritual life and then asked me if I would like to give myself to Christ.

I said, "YES", I would because for the first time in my life, I finally realized I needed God. I was still reeling from the blows that had come my way. I felt like life was cruel. I was down and out and feeling poorly about my children. Others knew it but could not help.

Here was finally someone who held out a ray of hope. So, that afternoon the minister came to our room, and we knelt and prayed.

No Damascus road as for Paul. Just a simple room at the Mission. But I know that for me it was great as it was for Paul. While I was praying, suddenly, my body felt like it was on fire, and I started to cry, and I know that God was working inside of me. I have never been able to explain how I felt at that moment. Something happened. It was real!

Like a blinding flash that overcame Paul on the Damascus road, I was overwhelmed at this moment. It was the desperateness of my situation.

My past life apart from Jesus Christ, what had happened to my marriage, and losing my children to foster homes, all this closed in on me at this moment. I was a nervous wreck. The minister at the mission brought hope to my life. God, through Jesus Christ, brought salvation. The children went back to their foster homes after Christmas. I went to Massachusetts to try and rebuild my life.

A new life was possible. Now I was a Christian, a follower of Jesus. There I had my parents to help me, but my real break came when my sister-in-law introduced me to the Pastor and his wife at a Baptist church in Massachusetts.

They mean a great deal to me and played a significant part in the shaping of my life as a Christian, a follower of Jesus. Finding an immediate acceptance from the pastor and the congregation, I became a member and, also, joined the Young Adult group and fully immersed myself in the congregation's life.

This experience meant much to me in terms of my acceptance as a human being. I had known years of rejection and alienation without the approval of me as a husband and father. In the church, I found out what was lacking. My worth as a child of God became clear in my eyes.

The church is God's reconciling agent in the world—to bring healing to humanity. My nurture as a Christian continued with the help of that Baptist church, especially the pastor and his wife. They taught me the habit of prayer. I owe an awful lot to them. They were my spiritual womb, where I was nurtured as a babe in Christ. Being the humble people they were, they, of course, disclaim that they did anything for Howard Barrick. To Christ, be the glory!

With this new outlook on life, my second chance given by God, and the help of a congregation of Christians, I was ready to go back to a job.

So, I packed my bag and headed for Niagara Falls, New York and to my former employer, to seek employment. Thank you, Lord; I was rehired by that company for their location at the Quakertown, Pennsylvania plant. So, I went back home to Massachusetts to pack and bring all my personal belongings here. I arrived in Quakertown in September 1967—lonely, fearful of the future, and all alone in a strange place. I needed companionship, so I sought it out in a logical place - the church.

I had one bad experience with a marriage partner, so I was determined that I would never marry again unless I could find the best possible Christian woman. That is precisely what happened. I met Marian through a mutual friend, and my courtship blossomed into marriage.

My life had taken a decided turn for the better. As I reflect upon what occurred, I think many times of that marvelous experience at the mission in Niagara Falls on Christmas Day. God and I found each other just when I needed Him most. Now I realize what I had missed for so many years without Christ as my Savior. From that moment, life was different—not necessarily more comfortable, merely different.

With the assistance of the people from the Baptist church, I grew in my Christian experience and in my determination to marry a Christian. It was not easy. Most of you cannot realize that it is <u>hard</u> being a born again Christian when you have not been a Christian all your life.

Some of you, reading this, may have grown up in Christian families and the church. For converts to Christianity, the temptation to wander is tempting; to slip back to use rough language, to wanting to be one of the boys. But my new associations in the church helped me. Paul, on the Damascus Road, met his Savior in a moment. In a blinding flash of light, the course of his life was changed. It was a dynamic experience that transformed him.

That was how I met Jesus Christ, in a mission room, in Niagara Falls, and in just a moment, it was a sudden transforming experience that turned my life around. Many Christians do not have such a dynamic experience. But the total surrendering experience can be as real, and this is just the way it happened to me.

In the experience of many, becoming a Christian, it can usually be a slow, thought-filled process taking many years. They grow in the knowledge and understanding of the faith until one day they stop and say, "The Christian way—this is the right way for me." For most of you, this is how you become a Christian, a follower of Jesus Christ.

After growing up in a Christian family, there came the day when you said "Yes" to Jesus Christ in Confirmation. Neither way is better—the slow thought-filled process like Timothy or the sudden conversion like Paul. They are both real.

That I am a born-again Christian, I have no doubt. You are just as sure of your faith. Jesus Christ can remake people. He can make us into the people God would want us to be.

Because of what I have been through in an unfortunate marriage, the breaking of my family, a troubling of the spirit, and then the subsequent re-orientation of my life in Christ, I feel a closeness and a devotion to God. I have seen the hand of God at work. That God provided Marian for me, I have no doubt. For this, I am grateful. I feel that we are directed to find each other within the mysterious providence of God at work.

Now I am genuinely loved; genuinely accepted for what I am as a human being. My life is being restored. My family is coming back together again. I have a good Christian wife.

Because of what has happened to me, I have a deep sense of gratitude to God and the church. Out of that gratitude, I have a deep desire to work for the Kingdom of God and the church; to evidence my feelings; my sense of belonging.

That ought to be every man's ambition. To work for God and His church out of a sense of gratitude. God has done so much for us. We ought to be willing to do our "little" for Him.

Let us pray:

O God stop us short in going our own way.

Turn us around to serve Thee and to do Thy will. We pray in Jesus' blessed name. Amen

May God bless you and your families,
Howard

18. Knowing that you were not redeemed with corruptible things, like silver or gold, from your aimless conduct received by tradition from your fathers,

19. But with the precious blood of Christ, as of a lamb without blemish and without spot.

20. He indeed was foreordained before the foundation of the world, but was manifest in these last times for you.

Thomas R. Hamilton
personal story

I came from a religious family. My grandfather was a missionary in what is now North Korea. My father was born in Korea and spent his first two decades there.

His brothers and sisters all became either pastors or missionaries or married one, so I always went to Sunday School and church. I knew all the stories and never doubted their truth. I would often attend summer Bible camps for most years. I would frequently respond to evangelists' messages and "walked the aisle" for Billy Graham, just to mention one, and even a woman missionary who came home on leave. But I was an unchanged rotten kid getting into trouble and never saw what the Bible talks about - a life change.

NKJV 2 Corinthians 5:17- "Therefore, if anyone is in Christ, *he is* a new creation; old things have passed away; behold, all things have become new."

By the time I was in Junior High, I was pretty much content with a worldly life. I enjoyed my new friends and rebellious lifestyle. I loved the world's rock music, soon adopted its immorality standards, and eventually got into an assortment of drugs and alcohol.

The summer after I turned sixteen, my parents 'sentenced' me to a Christian camp one more time as a last-ditch effort to salvage their kid. I had an uncle who was a Baptist pastor, it was he that recommended the camp. Having been down that road before, I knew what to expect at the camp. I would argue with the counselors about the Bible doctrines.

You see, I knew enough of the Bible to make me dangerous. But strangely, every argument I raised, and every objection I posed was gently and patiently answered according to the Word of God. I thought I had my counselor stumped when I raised an issue that he said he did not know the answer to but that he would find out.

When he came back later with an answer, that shattered the final feeble wall I had built around myself, and I knew I could resist no longer. I had always believed the truth of the Bible but was unwilling to yield myself to its authority.

Strangely, I had always intended to become a Christian when I was twenty-six, figuring that by then, I would have tasted all that the world had to offer. I thought I had my life planned, and this 'God thing' figured out.

I thought I had all my bases covered until I discovered

this: The rich man's life was snuffed out unexpectedly, and he ended up in fires of damnation. NKJV Luke 12:20-21 ...20 "But God said to him, Fool! This night your soul is required of you; then whose will those things be which you have provided? 21. So is he who lays up treasure for himself, and is not rich toward God."

There was no guarantee that I would ever reach age twenty-six. NKJV 2 Corinthians 6:2 "For He says: *"In an acceptable time I have heard you, and in the day of salvation I have helped you."* Behold now is the accepted time; behold, now is the day of salvation."

I had no trouble believing I was a hell-deserving sinner. NKJV Romans 6:23- "For the wages of sin *is* death, but the gift of God is eternal life in Christ Jesus our Lord."

I knew that I had to bow my knee to Jesus and receive Him as my Savior.

NKJV John 1:12-13, 12. "But as many as received Him, to them He gave the right to become children of God, to those who believe in his name: 13. who were born, not of blood, nor the will of the flesh, nor of the will of man, but of God."

So, that Monday morning, while sitting on a tree stump with two counselors sitting at my feet, I repented of my sins and asked Jesus to save me. And you know what? *He did.*

He began changing me right away. I flushed the drugs down the toilet that day. I called my mom and, for the first time in years, told her I loved her. I asked her if I could stay longer at camp.

Joyfully and tearfully, she agreed. I had enough money in my pocket to purchase some illegal drugs to begin selling it with a friend, but instead, I used the money to pay for my second week of camp. I called my girlfriend and asked her to come up to camp. She did, and I began to share Jesus with her as soon as I saw her.

She later got saved that night. (She is now my wife of over four decades.) Those two weeks of the camp became five weeks while I drank in the teachings of the Word. The Lord began to change me. He gave me a hunger for His Word that has never gone away. He began to change my life from the inside out.

My senior year in high school became a proving ground for my new faith. The Bozo courses I had chosen to drift through the rest of high school, I scrapped and ramped up to a full, more responsible load that would push me into a different direction.

Though I witnessed to my old friends, they soon drifted away from me since my faith no longer coincided with their choices. I found new friends who walked with the Lord. I started a Bible study.

The knowledge I gained at camp whet my appetite for more. I applied to a one-year Bible Institute, thinking that the Bible was not that big and that I could master it in a year.

Graduating from high school, I went to the Bible

Institute and soon learned that the Bible was an infinitely deep Book and would take longer to grasp it fully. I then applied to a Bible College and graduated from it, not wholly mastering the Word, but equipped with the tools and desire to feed my hunger for the rest of my life.

My new wife and I began to learn firsthand the truth of the Scriptures, where it says in NKJV Psalm 37:23, "The steps of a good man are ordered by the Lord, and He delights in his way."

The Lord allowed me to teach Bible and physical science in a Christian School for three years. The seventh, through tenth-grade students, stretched my faith and drove me deeper and deeper into the Word to find answers that would satisfy both them and me. I realized that the Lord was leading me to pursue ordination into a pastoral ministry.

For eight years, I enjoyed being an associate pastor and principal of a Christian school. After that school folded, I became a senior pastor in New Jersey for fifteen years and then pastored a church in Kansas for over twelve years.

Now? God continues to lead and tweak my life's direction. I have found peace ministering to those approaching the end of their lives as I work as a chaplain in a hospice ministry, giving comfort, guidance, and counsel to the infirmed and their families.

My wife has given me five precious daughters who walk with the Lord. They have each found husbands who share their passion for serving Him. They have given us fifteen (so far) grandchildren who are being reared in nurture and admonition of the Lord.

Have you ever experienced salvation in your life? Do you know if you were to die this instant, whether you would spend eternity in Heaven?

Would you like to know Jesus as your Savior?

NKJV Titus 3: 5-7

5: Not by works of righteousness which we have done, but according to His mercy He saved us, through the washing of regeneration and renewing of His Holy Spirit.

6: whom He poured out on us abundantly through Jesus Christ our Savior,

7: that having been justified by His grace we should become heirs according to the hope of eternal life.

Mike O'Hare personal story

Hello and blessings in the name of the Lord Jesus Christ!!!
My name is Mike O'Hare and I have lived all my days
in the Lehigh Valley area in the state of Pennsylvania,
USA. The Lehigh Valley is a growing area and is almost
directly in between Philadelphia and New York. There
are many families (like mine) who have lived in the area
for generations as well as many first-generation families
moving into this area of the USA.

The spiritual needs and opportunities in the Lehigh
Valley are great with a clear need for new Bible teaching
churches reaching out to the unchurched and under
churched.

I came to faith in Jesus Christ in my early twenties
as a direct result of the witness of my wife, Leslie. As I
reflect on my decision to trust in Jesus for my salvation,
I would describe it as more of a process than a singular
event.

Over the course of several years I can see how God
was drawing me into a personal relationship with Him.

However, the most influential witness to me about the need to trust Jesus and become His follower was my wife, Leslie. Her patient and unyielding witness along with the confidence that she belonged to God was something that I had never seen in anyone.

Being raised in the Roman Catholic tradition; attending Roman Catholic schools and seminary taught me a great deal about spiritual truths and traditions. There was always a spiritual interest on my part, however, I did not understand the basic truth of the Gospel: Salvation is not what I do for God rather salvation means receiving by faith what Jesus has completed for me.

This central truth seems truly clear to me now (after almost forty years of following Jesus) but, as I said, it was a process.

Salvation does not end with a one-time decision to follow Jesus. Salvation is something that I must receive by faith every day. Not only will God save me from eternal punishment in a place called Hell, He also wants to save me daily from sin as I learn how to live by faith and walk in the power of the Holy Spirit. I want to serve Him not out of obligation but with complete gratitude for His saving work in my life. Hallelujah!!!

As a follower of Jesus there has always been a "hunger and thirst" for more. Reading, studying, and memorizing Scripture are all things that bring deep satisfaction as well as transformative power into my life. In so many ways I have only "scratched the surface" of God's majesty.

As a follower of Jesus, I want everyone to hear about the opportunity for Salvation. There is an urgent need in this area of the USA for good Bible teaching churches that are focused on the unchurched and under churched. The Bible teaches that the local church is the hope of the world as it expresses itself with the diversity of gifts by the Holy Spirit.

Thank you,

Mike

NKJV Acts 2: 38-39

38. Then Peter said to them, "Repent, and let every one of you be baptized in the name of Jesus Christ for the remission of sins; and you shall receive the gift of the Holy Spirit."

39. For the promise is for you and your children, and to all who are afar off, as many as the Lord our God will call."

Jessica's personal story

I sat in a church my whole life and heard of Jesus but did not know Jesus!!

I know this is a common problem we have in our churches today. And we need to talk about it more!! We need to talk about the fact there are Christians who go to church every Sunday but are not born-again. We need to talk about how churches are full of members but empty in conversions. How do I know we have this problem? Because I was one of those lost sheep that went to church every Sunday.

I sat in the chair of a church my whole life. Some Sundays, I listened, and some Sundays, I was so distracted that the pastor could have called me by name, and I would not have noticed.

My mother, a Christian, forced me to come in hopes that her only daughter would find the same God she knew.

We attended different Christian churches, some that told the true gospel, and then gave a worthless motivational speech that only tickled our ears. Thank the Lord, some of those Gospel seeds landed on good soil in my heart and finally gave fruits.

I was born on June 14th, 1990, in El Paso, Texas. As soon as my adolescent years came, I lived recklessly. I did drugs, hung out with gangsters, and even landed in juvenile detention. I became pregnant when I was sixteen, and it was then I decided to make better choices for the sake of my innocent child, born in 2007. Smartest choice, at that time, was for me to join the U.S. Army, when I was nineteen years old, to escape my situation.

Once we moved away, my family and I were doing better in terms of what the world calls living better, but I was still lost in the darkness of sin. When I was not working, I was at the club drowning in alcohol and bad relationships. Living my best life is what they call it today.

I was in my pride and felt hatred towards people who had hurt my family and me. I was smoking like a chimney; about a pack a day. I did not understand how lost I was, and I thought I was only doing what everyone at my age did. I even remember saying once that God was for older adults and that I would come to God after I had my fun first.

When I was twenty-four years old and still in the army, I was stationed at Fort Steward, Georgia, and living with my mother and only son. I was then only a few weeks away from relocating to Alaska.

I was scrolling through the internet when a random video popped up on my related topics. It was titled "Warning to Christians." For some reason, this intrigued me because I considered myself a Christian. I listened to the hour-long video, and something in me began to stir for the first time. I was engulfed in terrible fear like somehow I knew that my time had come to make a choice. I knew I was living a life of fornication and drunkenness, and if I continued to list my sins, we would be writing a book.

I knew I was on the wrong path. I knew that the life I was living was everything the God I claimed to know hated. I knew it, and I think that is what made it worse for me. Everything became very real to me when I heard that pastor warning Christians, "hell would be full of us lukewarm Christians who love doing the pleasures of the world more than living for our Lord." It felt like he was talking to me. I felt like death was knocking at my door. It was a very surreal moment that even today I do not understand why it happened that day and not before.

That night I grabbed my mother and son and told them we need to pray. My mother was surprised to say the least, but she did not hesitate. I gave my life to Jesus Christ that night on my living room floor.

I can remember all the words to my prayer too.

I remember I told Jesus that I was tired of living my life for me and that I was ready to *surrender* everything over to Him.

I surrendered all my desires and everything I loved doing to Him, knowing that I might lose some of the things I wanted. But I did not care because, at that moment, I wanted Jesus more than anything else.

I also prayed for something that did not make sense to me because it was a weird thing to ask for, especially coming out of my mouth. I was so sincere in my prayer that I figured it was from the heart. I asked Jesus for a new heart. I asked Jesus for a new heart because I felt my current heart was too broken and dark for Him to do anything useful with it. Later that year I found in NKJV Ezekiel 36:26, "I will give you a new heart and put a new spirit within you; I will take the heart of stone out of your flesh and give you a heart of flesh." I also later read that the Holy Spirit intercedes for us in NKJV Romans 8:26-27. 26. "Likewise the Spirit also helps in our weaknesses. For we do not know what we should pray for as we ought, but the Spirit Himself makes intercession for us with groanings which cannot be uttered. 27. Now he who searches the hearts knows what the mind of the Spirit is, because He makes intercession for the saints according to the will of God."

I, without a doubt, believe that the Holy Spirit was interceding in my prayer because that was my first time praying with a sincere heart.

I had to get to that place where I was willing to let Him touch everything He wanted in my life without limiting Him, and that was the first time I was actually in that place in my heart. The next day I prayed and told Jesus I wanted to know where to start.

So, I started reading the Bible and came to NKJV Matthew 6:15 where Jesus said, *"But if you do not forgive men their trespasses, neither will your Father forgive your trespasses."* When I read that, I thought of all the sins that I needed Jesus Christ to forgive me for, and without hesitation, I knew I wanted to let go of the hate in my heart, not for their sake but for mine.

I felt in my heart that I needed to call certain people from my past and apologize to them. At first, when these people came to my mind, I smirked and told God they should be asking me for an apology. But I did it anyway because I felt this was how I needed to start. I called, and they were all gracious and accepted my apology. Then I called my ex-sister-in- law, who I had not spoken to in years. When I got through apologizing to her, she apologized to me and told me she found Jesus, too. We rejoiced together on the phone, and that was when I saw what a blessing forgiveness has been to me and really began to fuel my faith.

I saw what Jesus did in my ex-sister-in-law and how different she was from the woman I had known years before. I could hear the change in her even over the phone. I was so excited, when I got off the phone, that I told Jesus whatever it was He was doing in her life, I wanted Him to do in mine too.

I had a church friend who I respected because I really

felt she was a genuine Christian. I asked her where she would recommend that I start reading, and she told me to start with the New Testament of the Bible. Before I began to read, I would pray and ask God to help me understand its secrets. Let me tell you, brothers and sisters... the Bible opened up to me like a children's book. Every word captivated me, and the more I read, the more I wanted to read.

I felt God with me through every page I turned. I had such a craving to keep reading and never stop. I loved His Word plus watching and listening to people's testimonies on various sites of the internet.

The more I read, the hungrier I got. I thought it was amazing that a person without a degree in Theology was able to understand the Bible. I could feel my heart changing the closer I got to Him. I would get on my hands and knees after I read something that reminded me of my sin, and I would weep and repent.

That became my favorite place to be, on my knees, talking to Jesus. I felt like I was on a honeymoon with my Saviour. I felt like nothing could hurt me. I felt the most powerful, yet comforting, love I have ever felt in my life. I felt all this love from someone I could not see, but I could feel without a single doubt in my mind.

As the Holy Spirit began to unfold the Bible to me, my desires began to change. Suddenly I am not interested in clubbing, drinking, or dressing the same way. Jesus and His love were satisfying me in a way that the world had never been able to fill me up before. I loved this feeling of fullness and did not want anything to come in between my God and me.

I finished the New Testament, and then I reread it, and again. Each time I read it, I discovered new things. After I read the New Testament maybe four times, I decided I was probably ready for the Old Testament.

Jesus became my Pastor and the Holy Spirit, my teacher. They were teaching me, leading me, and convicting me. If I had a question about what I was reading, I would ask the Lord, and He would reveal to me His Holy Scriptures. Jesus never left me wondering or lost. He was always there to answer my questions when I had them.

"But the anointing which you received from Him abides in you, and you do not need that anyone teach you; but as the same anointing teaches you concerning all things, and is true, and is not a lie, and just as it has taught you, you will abide in Him.". (NKJV 1John: 2:27)

It has been the most amazing experience in my life what I have experienced with an open Bible, and I used to jump out of planes for a living (Army Airborne).

Then I read, in the Bible, about the baptism. I found a Christian church, and I was baptized in the name of Jesus Christ. That was the last day I smoked a cigarette. That was the sin I had struggled the most in letting go. Not that I did not want to, trust me, I had the most profound conviction to let it go. If you have ever been a slave to nicotine, then you know what I mean.

The day before I got baptized, I prayed, and I told the Lord that I hated sin and that I wanted to be a good testimony of what His power and amazing love can do in the most wretched. I prayed and asked the Lord to help leave my cigarette addiction once and forever, and that is what the Lord did.

I was baptized in a lake in Alaska in the month of July. It was freezing cold, but I wanted nothing more than to make a public display of who I was walking with, Jesus Christ. I wanted Satan and the demons that used to live with me to see who my God and King was.

I wanted to show the world what God had done on the inside. "Therefore, if anyone is in Christ, he is a new creation; old things passed away; behold, all things have become new." (NKJV 2 Corinthians 5:17).

Being Born Again is REAL!! Jesus answered and said to him, "most assuredly, I say to you, unless one is born again, he cannot see the kingdom of God." (NKJV John 3:3)

My testimony goes deeper and is still not over. If I went into every amazing miracle and transformation in my life, I would be writing a book as thick as the Bible. God is REAL. What He did in me, He can do in you and anyone willing to surrender.

I want you, the reader, to understand the woman who now knows Jesus Christ. I was dreadful, vile, and hateful. I was the chief of sinners. Like Paul said in NKJV 1Timothy 1:15, "this is a faithful saying and worthy of all acceptance, that Christ Jesus came into the world to save sinners, of whom I am chief."

I ran from God for so many years, not only because I loved my sin, but also because I felt that God wanted nothing to do with a woman like me. I thought I had to be a good woman, or this or that, before He would accept me. I did not know or understand God's holiness and sovereignty.

You can begin to see how lost we are, no matter what your perception of sin is. Whether you sold your soul to the devil or you stole a candy from the grocery store, when we break one law, we are guilty of breaking them all. (read NKJV James 2:10)

We desperately need Jesus Christ, and there is no other route to salvation, but through Jesus Christ. (read NKJV John 14:6)

There is nobody so filthy or so lost that Jesus Christ cannot come and turn your world right-side up. Neither is there anyone so righteous or so good that they do not need Jesus Christ.

If we say that we have no sin, we deceive ourselves, and the truth is not in us. (NKJV 1John 1:8) *I have not come to call the righteous, but sinners to repentance.* (NKJV Luke 5:32) *For the Son of Man has come to seek and to save that which was lost.* (NKJV Luke 19:10)

I left scriptures throughout my testimony so the

reader, whether saved or lost, can open the Bible, and read the scriptures that saved my life and, more importantly, my soul.

Each scripture scattered throughout my testimony pertains to that moment in my life. God bless the reader, whoever it may be. I pray that my testimony may be a blessing and a testimony of what the power of Jesus Christ can do for the lost. God Bless!

"And they overcame him by the blood of the Lamb and by the word of their testimony, and they did not love their lives to the death."

(NKJV Revelation 12:11)

"For the word of God is LIVING and powerful, and sharper than any two-edged sword, piercing even to the division of soul and spirit, and of joints and marrow and is a discerner of the thoughts and intents of the heart."

(NKJV Hebrews 4:12)

Thank you,

Jessica

NKJV 2 Corinthians 5:20-21

20. Now then, we are ambassadors for Christ, as though God were pleading through us; we implore *you* on Christ's behalf, be reconciled to God.

21. For He made Him who knew no sin *to be* sin for us, that we might become the righteousness of God in Him

Kevin's personal story

When I was younger my mom used to take me to church. She would dress me up, and we would go past my buddies down the street, and they would laugh at me.

I did not want to go; I would give her a hard time about going. When I was young, I would go to church only because my mom would make me.

We went to a Presbyterian church. As I got older, I drifted away from the church, and then I started to hang out with some bad guys and was reckless. I did my own thing then, partying and stuff. I got into some trouble at that time so this was a wakeup call. I knew I had to change my life. I needed to settle down. So, I got married and started a family. I still did not have a relationship with God at this point - was just doing my own thing!

I started doing DJ jobs and some bars plus partying. I was married for twenty-five years, and things were rocky. My wife and I were going through trials and tribulations, and I wanted to seek some counseling.

Where I worked, there was a minister, and I wanted him to counsel us. I would go, but my wife did not think she needed to go. Neither one of us were saved.

As time went on, I just dealt with it and fought through it even though it was a tough and rocky marriage. When time went on, and things got even rougher, I said, "I've got to go back to church!".

I had a cousin and he attended church. I think he was going as a regular Sunday obligation, but I do not believe he was saved either. So, here I was going to church again, and went for a while but then fell away from it. Then things seemed to be better with the wife, I went back home but, eventually, picked up the same routine. Then it got to the point of being hopeless and I was tired and said I am done and got a divorce.

Now I wanted to change. One day I was sitting in the car, and I scanned my radio and started listening to the **Word**. Listened to a minister and he was preaching about surrendering, to surrender in everything and let God lead and guide you. I thought about it, and I said that is what I am going to do... surrender.

I am tired of doing things Kevin's way!

So, when the minister explained the plan of salvation, what we should do to be saved, I did that. I asked God to come in and change my life. I wanted to listen to His voice.

People told me that if you just quiet your spirit, you can hear God speak to you. So, one day I went to my room, and I shut everything down, then I asked him to talk to me. I just quieted my spirit and asked him to use me, and He said, "I will use you." From that day, the Lord has shown me mighty and great things.

He has really done some impressive things in my life.

I did not know how to pray. I used to get together with my co-workers and they would pray, but I did not even know what to say. I learned by watching and listening to them. When God told me that he would use me, I was a little afraid because I did not know His Word. I did not know much about it either. But he said to me that he would send someone that will help teach me. I met a guy who knew a lot from the Bible, who preached. He worked with me and lived in an employee apartment of one of the residential buildings. What an influence he was to me!

There was also another co-worker that prayed with the two of us. We were able to get together and pray several times each week. I asked God to show me how to pray, and before I knew it, I was really praying! Prayers are like having a conversation with God. Prayers are powerful. When we got together and prayed, I saw the fruit by workings in my family.

He showed me how much He loved us, and I saw a lot of change in my life and how powerful He is. Some people I used to be with just drifted away. I felt that God wanted me to spend a lot of time with Him just seeking and searching for Him, and that is what I did. I spent a lot of time on my knees, and the more I pressed in on Him, I felt Him pressing on me.

Let me show you how powerful prayer is. One of my co-workers was going through a tough time in her marriage, and he gave her strength. Then she lost that husband and faced hard times. God strengthened her through that time. We kept on praying. She never wanted to get married again, but God brought a special man into her life. He himself became a believer after we met him and they ended up getting married.

God gave me strength when I had to face the death of my father. God and I had a close relationship, and he gave me peace at that time. He put men and women of God around me to help me grow in my relationship with Jesus Christ, and I just thank God for all that.

Now I pray God will work in my children in their lives and to realize where I was and where I am today. I just really, really appreciate what God has done in my life and what is to come.

Thank you, Lord. My favorite verse is:

"For God so loved the world, that He gave His only begotten son, that whoever believes in Him shall not perish, but have everlasting life."

NKJV John 3:16

May God bless you and your family,

Kevin

NKJV Titus 2:11-12 11. For the grace of God that brings salvation has appeared to all men. 12. Teaching us that, denying ungodliness and worldly lust, we should live soberly, righteously, and godly in the present age,

NKJV Luke 19:10 "for the son of man has come to seek and to save that which was lost."

My name is Dellbo
(stage name)

I grew up in a suburb of Detroit. Since there were not many kids that lived near me, I was allowed to have a paper route at age eight with eleven customers. After a year or two, the newspaper company was purchased by a larger newspaper corporation. So, my paper route grew to sixty plus customers before I was twelve years old. I share this because I enjoyed making my own money at such a young age. Money is good, but as you read on, it shows that it can bring sorrow as well.

I attended a Lutheran school from grades one through eight. Each day the first one and a half hours of school was religious training where we recited Bible verses, sang hymns, studied the catechism, and learned religious history.

During my seventh and eighth grades, I appeared on a TV quiz show against other Lutheran schools in the Metropolitan Detroit area. Seventh graders usually did not make the four-person team, but I did. I knew a lot of stuff, people, etc.

I knew all the right things about Jesus, His virgin birth, His death on the cross, resurrection, coming again, etc. I went to church almost every Sunday and obviously considered myself a Christian.

I went to church almost every Sunday as a seventeen and eighteen-year-old but was hung over the majority of the time. I did not pay attention to what was being preached, the hymns, etc., but I always waited until the end, and faithfully listened to the benediction where the minister would grant God's peace.

So, I wanted peace and truth in my life like everyone else, but I had a hole in my heart...one that I was anesthetizing with alcohol.

I began my journey drinking alcohol as a young teenager. Years passed, and I did not drink any less; in fact, the drinking escalated, it always does. I discovered I was going to be a father at age twenty-one, and my girlfriend was nineteen. We married and had three wonderful children in 1968, 1972 and 1976.

I really loved my children's mother, but my drinking grew, and I added marijuana to the mix. I considered myself a high-a-holic, and six out of seven days of the week I was either stoned or drunk.

Unfortunately, the marriage officially ended in 1985, although we were separated in 1980. We remain friends, and I have admitted to her that it was 95% my fault.

On Christmas Eve 1980, I was at a jewelry store waiting for a bracelet to be engraved for my 1968 daughter. While waiting for what seemed like an awfully long time, I bought a bottle of alcohol and smoked several marijuana cigarettes.

Driving on the way to my house that I was not living at, I decided to walk nine holes at a local golf course to sober up. I almost made it there, but unfortunately, a slippery dusting of snow on the roadway caused me to do a 180°, and I hit a bridge going backward, which sheared off the back of the car.

A police officer put me in his squad car, drove me home, and carried me into the house where I had once lived with my family. I received no citation to my surprise. The vehicle was leased, and, unbelievably, I was released from the lease contract with no monies due.

We went to a church as a family (unbelievably) the Sunday after Christmas. I was moved by the worship service and had to suppress walking forward. My wife, unfortunately, hated it. She has never become a Christian.

I wrote on the back of the welcome card that I would like to speak with the pastor. On January 6, two deacons from the church came to my house as I was babysitting at the time.

Naturally, I offered them an alcoholic drink that was turned down. We spoke for a while, and I asked if I might be able to speak with the pastor.

On January 13, the pastor showed up and we both

drove our cars to a restaurant about 200 yards from where I was living with a friend. We chatted about a variety of things, and then he asked me the question: "If you were to die tonight, would you spend eternity in Heaven?" I responded, "I hope so." He then asked, "if there was a way to know for sure, would that be something that would interest you?" I said absolutely, yes!

He immediately read NKJV 1 John 5:13 where it says, *"these things I have written to you who believe in the name of the Son of God, that you may know that you have eternal life, and that you may continue to believe in the name of the Son of God."* I read and reread that verse for two to three minutes. I could not believe that you could know, I was blown away.

Throughout my life, my Lutheran pastors had never mentioned the certainty of eternal life. This pastor told me what to pray, and I left the restaurant. I drove the 200 yards, ran upstairs, got down on my knees, asked the Lord to forgive me of my many sins, to come into my heart, and be my Savior and Lord.

I knew that Jesus was the Savior, but I was never saved. I asked him to take over my life and be my Lord. I give up. I have messed up my entire thirty-four years of existence. I surrender. *He did and I was saved!*

Have the last thirty-nine years been free of problems? Certainly not. But I have had perfect peace plus the peace of God that passes all understanding.

I remarried in 1986. As the Lord says in his Word if

the unbeliever departs, let them depart, and he allowed me to remarry. I had previously led wife number two to the Lord. It was a very rocky marriage, and walking on eggshell was the norm. That marriage ended up in a divorce, as well.

I met my current wonderful wife in the church, and we were married in 2004. God has redeemed, forgiven, and blessed us. I have been the church administrator for the past eleven plus years, and I have been on twelve evangelism trips to Cuba since 2006.

God delivered me from marijuana two months after I was saved. He delivered me from the bondage of nicotine in 1988. He allowed me to struggle with alcohol until May 2012. Praise God that he never gave up on me, and I will be eight years free in May of 2020.

My life is saturated with His love, and He has taught me so many things through the ministry of new life, to celebrate recovery and the life recovery Bible.

My goal is to serve Him until I am free of this horrible sin nature that every person struggles with to one degree or another. This is what happens when the Holy Spirit dwells in you. He guides you through life during your weakest moments.

I hope you understand that no one has done anything that He is unwilling to forgive and grant them a new life in Him, amen.

Thank you and may God bless you.

NKJV 1 Peter 1:8-9 8. Whom having not seen you love. Though now you do not see Him, yet believing, you rejoice with joy inexpressible and full of glory. 9. Receiving the end of your faith-the salvation of your souls.

NKJV Hebrews 9:28 so Christ was offered once to bear the sins of many. To those who eagerly await Him He will appear a second time, apart from sin, for salvation.

Pastor Larry's personal story

My story is probably best told from the perspective of hindsight; it goes way back. I used to think that my account was not worth mentioning because it was not overly exciting; it was not dramatic; it was not a "gutter to glory" kind of story. Then I realized that in many ways, it was one of the most powerful stories because it is about God saving me from the impact of sin.

It goes back to my beginning. I was born into a family where my mom and dad both loved Jesus Christ and went to church. At the earliest opportunity, probably several weeks old, my parents took me to church, and we continued going. Since that early age, I never knew anything but going to church. And it was a church that preached the Bible as truth, the whole truth, and nothing but the truth.

I grew up hearing that Jesus was the only way to God, from as early as I could understand the message. And I will say that as a little kid, it was easy for me to see that I had done bad things. Yes, I had disobeyed my parents. Yes, I lied about things or had pushed my brother or something else that was bad. So, it was not hard to convince me that I was a sinner.

It also was not hard to convince me that God loved me. I had parents that loved me, and I was in a safe environment. It was easy to see God as someone who loved me. So, when the preacher said, "who wants to go to heaven someday?"… well, as little kid, it was kind of like going to the candy store. Of course, I wanted to go to heaven! So why wouldn't I ask Jesus to save me?

I probably prayed that prayer five or more times between the age of five and eight. Perhaps after a Sunday morning service or with a Sunday school teacher or summertime VBS (Vacation Bible School). So, when did God write my name in the book of life? I do not know for sure. I do not know which of those prayers He took as the genuine one. I only know that at the age of eight, I sat down with my parents and said, "I want to get baptized!".

My dad sat me down, and we talked through the gospel and the story of Jesus one more time, and I prayed one more time that Jesus would forgive my sins and be my Savior.

Well, that was not the end of my story.

I look back on it and say, yes, I am sure that I was saved at that point. I also remember when I was about twelve years old, I started thinking more like a teenager.

I began to see girls differently, I started to see my friends and peer pressure from a different perspective, and I started to doubt my salvation. How could I really be saved if I think these thoughts, if I am struggling with these issues? How can a person like that really be saved? So, I talked with my pastor. He just recounted the gospel. And I said yes, I believe all that. And he said, then you are already saved.

Being saved does not mean you have all the answers. It means you are "born-again" and you need to grow in your faith. Just like a baby does not run on their own right away: they grow, learn to crawl, walk, and then run. You learn to practice all these principles that Jesus saved you to practice and to live.

Here is the hindsight part of my story. When I look back at my teenage and young adult years, I remember watching many friends stumble and fall to peer pressure. They stumbled with social compromise, getting involved with drugs, driving drunk and getting girls pregnant, and other issues that I was not directly involved.

I look back at some of that and wonder why I did not go there, why did I not stumble in some of these areas. The answer is not because I was good. The answer is not because I was righteous or holy. The answer was that I found Jesus at a young age, and He not only saved me from the penalty of my sin but also saved me from stumbling from some of the crimes (sins) that my friends had chosen to do.

I had read the Scriptures and studied God's principles. I had grown in His teaching concerning truth, living a disciplined life, walking away from the temptations and the will of the flesh.

I had mentors in my life (my parents, Sunday school teachers, and Christian leaders) who showed me how to follow Jesus' teaching rather than the world's teaching.

And I watched my friend's struggle. One girl did not graduate from high school because she became pregnant. One lost his life to drugs. Others made it into college but did not become successful in their lives because of self-centered lifestyles.

I look back on my salvation as a young boy and the mentoring of a biblical church and godly parents, and I realize that all the teachings of God's Word grew me in my salvation. Not that I did not make enough of my own mistakes, but I was able to be saved from many of my friend's mistakes because God rescued me at a young age.

When I look back, I realize my salvation was not only understanding and accepting that God saved me from the penalty of my sins. It was not just about hell and heaven. It was also that He made my path successful through living His principles. I was able to learn those principles as a young person.

My story is dramatic in that he rescued me from ever going through those dark places. And when I look back, I am forever humbled and grateful that God rescued me, as a child, from falling in that wrong path.

Since then, His principles have allowed me to weather many trials. My father graduated to heaven when I was twenty-seven. At that time, my first child was one year old, and I remember looking at God and saying, "how could you take my father away at a time like this? If I ever needed you, it's now." I now see that His answer was to put my trust in Him. He has a plan for each and every one of us. And I did so, one day at a time. And God blessed me with four children that their mom and I were privileged to raise and introduce to Jesus so that they could be rescued from the effect of sin at a young age.

And at fifty-seven, God chose to take my wife home after thirty-six incredible years of marriage. And once again, I was at a crossroads. This time it was as if I was being reminded about all the teachings and principles from the Bible that I grew up with. Well, what other answer could I give, but yes. And it is as if He smiled at me and I knew I would follow His Word.

It has been eight years since that experience. And I am here today to testify that God has been 100% faithful to me in every way.

The fulfillment of His salvation in my life is not only for my soul for eternity but also to make me successful, productive, and happy in every step of my life through every circumstance.

My salvation is not just about getting me to heaven. It is getting me through this great adventure called life… joyfully and expectedly, with complete trust in the One who made it possible - my Lord and my Savior Jesus Christ.

NKJV Romans 5: 8

"But God demonstrates His own love toward us, in that while we were still sinners, Christ died for us."

NKJV Romans 10: 9

"that if you confess with your mouth the Lord Jesus and believe in your heart that God raised Him from the dead, you will be saved."

Joe Fox, Sr. Testimony

This is my testimony of becoming a believer, and follower, of Jesus Christ. "Born-Again."

My family moved around a lot from one small town to another in South New Jersey. I was the youngest of four, one sister and two brothers, my oldest brother being five years older.

My parents divorced when I was about five years old. Mom now had the responsibility of raising four kids in the sixties and seventies. This was a tough time in our country for women because it was customary for the man to be the only worker in the home to pay for bills. It also became normal to have many young rebellious attitudes at that time.

With little to no financial support, mom had the challenge of finding jobs in a man's world. Thankfully, she was successful. In fact, she took on two and three jobs at a time to make ends meet.

Mom saw to it that we attended a local church, a Roman Catholic church, that was nearby. The afterschool classes taught many excellent stories with strong moral values, and it was a place for us to be until mom came home from work.

At the age of twelve, I was confirmed in my Catholic religion and given the name of Patrick.

All was going well until the following year. As usual, the church offering envelopes were mailed to our home address, but this time an extra envelope was given to ask for money to help repair the church's steeple that was struck by lightning. I remember the feeling. I might as well have been struck by lightning myself. My heart was broken over this extra envelope that was sent to ask for money.

As a young teenager, I watched as mom returned from the many exhausting hours she worked. All I could think of was, "how could they ask my mom for money when she is struggling?" and "why aren't they here helping my mom?"

I stopped attending our church for about three years. I was just in limbo until the devil stepped in to fill the void. A student at a public school was freely handing out pot to smoke, and many students joined in. It did not take long for my life to spiral out of control by quitting school after my freshman year. I left home to live with, of all people, my irresponsible dad.

All that summer and three months into the school year amounted to six months of misery. My mom called me and said, "Joe, come home, and I will get you back in school." With much persistence and care, my mom got me back into school. I entered my sophomore year. I needed to make up a lot of schoolwork. Somehow I managed to win an award for the most improved student. All because of a mom's love and care for her kids. I graduated high school and then was married in 1979, at the age of twenty-five.

Unfortunately, I continued using drugs and alcohol and carried them into our marriage. Four years into our marriage, and we were so miserable! I remember our paperboy, Kenny, who would deliver our daily paper with a big smile.

He so irritated me! I was miserable, and he was happy. I would curse him out and be so rude to him, and he would just come back smiling and telling me about Jesus. Each Friday, he would come to our door and collect the fees for our newspaper. On one particular Friday I walked away wishing I could be happy like him.

To make matters more challenging, my grandfather called me and invited me to his church. Upon arriving for the morning church service, I noticed something. A lot of people welcomed me with the same smile that paperboy had on his face. This warm, genuine welcome had a significant impact on me.

I thought to myself I never had this at my church. My church was big and cold and had an echo in it when someone spoke. When he came out to speak, the preacher in this church stayed at the pulpit and spoke directly from the Bible. At the end of the service he gave an invitation to come forward. I said no thanks to that. I am not going to embarrass myself by going to the front.

Then I returned the following week to listen to the preacher more intently. They had the invitation time again, but I still refused to go forward. The next day, which was a Monday, I had the most miserable day of my life. What was going on? I could not concentrate on my job as a carpet installer.

Throughout the day I kept seeing the paperboy's smiling face, the warm welcome of those church members caring about me, and the Bible verse of NKJV John 14:6 "Jesus said to him, I am the way, the truth, and the life. No one comes to the Father except through me." And this verse, I remember, my grandfather would often quote to me. Finally, the preacher was sharing about Jesus, who died for my sins and rose again. I could not take it anymore!

When I came home, my wife and our two kids were not there. I rushed into my bedroom and fell on my knees for the first time in my life. I asked Jesus Christ to forgive me for the many sins that I have committed. I also believed in my heart that He died on that cross for me and then rose again in victory over sin and death.

It is so hard to put into words to describe that moment. There was this huge relief. A lot of weight was lifted from me. I sensed an immediate love and peace that was so awesome!

Then there was freedom like I never felt before. *I was saved!!!* I finally had a smile on my face like my paperboy and those older folks from my grandfather's church.

Again, words are just that, until someone believes God's Word, the Bible. In the Bible, God tells us that Jesus loves us and that He gave His life for us.

It also tells us that whoever believes in Him receives forgiveness of their sins and will have the peace and joy inside that only He can give.

The following are verses that may help you to think and maybe even want to look deeper into God's Word.

NKJV John 3:16-17 16. "For God so loved the world that He gave his only begotten Son, that whoever believes in Him should not perish, but have everlasting life. 17. For God did not send His Son into the world to condemn the world, but that the world through Him might be saved."

NKJV Romans 3:10 "as it is written, there is none righteous, no, not one;"

NKJV Romans 6:23 "for the wages of sin is death, but the gift of God is eternal life in Christ Jesus our Lord."

NKJV Romans 10: 9-13 9. "that if you confess with your mouth the Lord Jesus and believe in your heart that God raised Him from the dead, you will be saved. 10. "For with the heart one believes unto righteousness, and with the mouth confession is made unto salvation." 11. For the Scripture says, "Whoever believes on Him will not be put to shame." 12. For there is no distinction between Jew and Greek, for the same Lord over all is rich to all who call on Him. 13. For "whoever calls on the name of the Lord shall be saved."

Thank you,

Joe Fox, Sr.

NKJV 2 Corinthians 5: 17 "Therefore, if anyone is in Christ, *he is* a new creation; old things have passed away; behold, things have become new."

NKJV Romans 6: 23 "For the wages of sin is death, but the gift of God is eternal life in Christ Jesus our Lord."

The story of the 1st day of the rest of my life, by Monica Silva

Before having a relationship with Yeshua (Hebrew name for Jesus), I always felt a sense of emptiness in my heart. Something (actually, it was someone) was missing. I felt like I was incomplete. This was hard to understand since I grew up in a loving home.

Early on in life, I decided this emptiness would be filled with what I considered success was, by way of performance based on merit. My parents continually praised me for doing a satisfactory job in school, so I made it my life's mission to strive for the "A" grading in every test.

My goal was to make my family proud, and as a result, I developed pride in a self-righteous attitude. Happiness was driven by results, and I felt like I was in complete control of it. I attributed my good grades to the fact that I put in the hard work of studying. Everything in my life followed this formula: working hard equals reaping a reward. If things did not work out the way I expected, I took that as a lesson and worked harder the next time.

I used the same strategy for my faith. Thankfully, I had a head start since the existence of God was never in question. After observing and studying the complexity of the world we live in, I always knew there was a Designer behind the design.

I treated God like a vending machine. If I put in the right rituals at the right frequency, I felt I could manipulate God and hence, control the outcome. From my perspective, God was transactional. I put in the work, and God issued the reward.

If reciting a memorized prayer, a couple of times, did not grant me the desired outcome, I would then increase the frequency. If this did not work, I would employ other tactics, such as prayer beads, kneeling and lighting up votive candles in front of iconic statues and praying to the person that would correspond to a particular need. For instance, if I wanted protection, I would pray *directly* to St. Michael or to a guardian angel. I had several cards, similar to funeral memorial cards, that I referred to as cheat sheets. They had the picture of the saint on the front with the description of what he/she represents and the corresponding prayer written on the back. I did not understand the meaning of prayer and honestly was burdened by it.

I had never experienced an encounter with God, so

I believed I needed those material items to fabricate an emotional connection. In the same way children cling to a teddy bear when they miss their parents, I became attached to these religious idols in my life and held onto them for security.

I, totally, 100% believed my works would save me. I continued to work hard, pursuing a terminal degree, thinking this was the main goal in life. I was hyper-focused on myself, my life, and my dreams. I continued to pursue my academic studies while at the same time, began to feel like a robot. Earning good grades began to seriously stress me out, and attending church became boring.

My time at church turned stale, with the exception of the homily, and I had committed the entire Mass (service) to memory. The most alarming thing to me was that I felt the same exact way before a church service as I did after church.

There was no feeling in my faith, only doing and attending church once a week simply checked off my duty to God. I believed salvation, or entrance into heaven, was something you could earn or achieve, and I lived with this mentality for nineteen years.

I began to question my purpose in life. Did I, at nineteen years of age, learn everything there is to know about God? I started to question my motivation. What drives me? What happens if all my life goals are met, then what? For the first time in my life, I started to question, is there more to life than what I have been taught? When I began to ask questions, I was met with puzzled faces. The most common answer I received was, "it is what it is, this is life."

When questioning religious practices, I was answered with this question: "what's the matter with you?" My parents thought I was disrespectful for examining my religion. I was not trying to be rude; I was simply looking for the burden of proof.

But God, in His infinite wisdom, had a plan to reveal himself to me.

It was in autumn 2006. There was an event on my college campus that advertised free pizza and drinks. It was the inter-varsity Christian Fellowship that sponsored it. I could care less about who was paying for pizza, and my only objective was to get a free meal and head back to the library to study. When I arrived at the room, there was a young man at the front of the class with a guitar in his hands, and a young woman was standing next to him singing on the microphone.

I thought, oh my goodness, this is great—a concert. I can use a study break. I sat in the back row. The music was modern and hip. I saw some students with their hands lifted to the ceiling, and I thought that was so weird. I started listening to the words that were being sung, and to my surprise, there was a mention of God, His Son Jesus, and the Holy Spirit. During the song, I literally felt a surge of God's love and was completely overcome by it.

It was supernatural and something I had never, ever experienced before. It felt like I was being wrapped in a warm blanket.

Time stood still. I tried to focus on the man with the guitar and the woman singing, but my vision became blurry with the tears that were accumulating in my eyes. I could not remember the last time I had cried in a public place in front of strangers before. What was happening? As tears uncontrollably rolled down my face, I felt a weight was being lifted off my shoulders. Until that point, I did not even realize I had been weighed down. I wanted so badly to remain in that moment forever, so I stayed there, receiving God's love.

It felt like a purifying river within me that continued to flow. It was amazing. God became so real to me at that moment, almost tangible. The person next to me realized what had taken place and invited me to their next meeting. I went because, whatever took place, had sparked my attention.

The next meeting arrived, and the group leader began with prayer. I was looking around for a prayer book or pages to follow along but did not find any. She was praying from her heart.

Until that moment, I had never heard a person praying the way she was praying. She was having a conversation with God, and I was just listening in, and it was interesting. She was using plain, easy-to-understand words and was talking to God as if He was her best friend.

Growing up, I had been taught that prayer had to be presented to God in a specific format to remain respectful. This woman seemed to be breaking the rules. I listened in complete shock.

After she was finished talking to God, she discussed the reason *why* Jesus *willingly* went to the cross. It is possible that I heard this explanation before, but for the first time, I was *listening*. I realized, at that moment, that I had never fully understood the gospel. I knew Jesus died and resurrected; however, I did not know why or how these historical events applied to me. She then asked if anyone was ready to accept Jesus' redemptive work of the cross and make Jesus their Savior. I had never heard of this offering before in my entire life!

A rush of realization came upon me. I am not the one in control; God is. The wall of self-righteousness came crashing down, and I realized that I was a sinner and in desperate need of a Savior. I realized that I knew about Jesus, but I did not know Him *personally*. I realized how much I needed God and wanted more of his love.

In that sobering moment, I finally realized that God's Son is perfect, without sin, and He took my place on that cross. I repented of my sin and decided in my heart to surrender my life to God. That day, I began a personal relationship with Jesus. I prayed the prayer of salvation, and in that precious moment began *the first day of the rest of my life*.

Do you remember the very first time you put on a pair of corrective lenses for the people wearing glasses? Do you remember the realization that you were once living in a blurry world, and now you see things so clearly? Do you remember thinking, how could I have lived so long without seeing things as they truly are? This is how I would compare my experience after I gave my life to Yeshua. Instantly, I began to see everything so clearly.

For those with great vision, do you remember the time you put on 3D glasses and looked away from the movie screen, how blurry everything around appeared? This blur was my life before accepting Christ.

I had never realized I was previously living in a fog until the fog was gone. I began to understand the term born-again. I had this incredible joy within me that was unshakable, undeniable, and consistently there, regardless of my circumstances.

My worldview expanded, and I started having compassion for complete strangers, leading to a desire to care for them. I began to feel God's presence and his love frequently.

Every time I would cry out to God, He would give me a sign that He is with me. God is so faithful. There were many miracles I am privileged to have witnessed as a baby in Christ. God was doing a work in me and teaching me to trust Him with everything. It was great. Day and night, I experienced zero fear and zero worries.

I began craving the same music I have listened to at that fellowship meeting, and God brought me to a Christian radio station. I asked God to teach me more about His love, and immediately my appetite to read the Bible grew.

Astonishingly, I had never owned a Bible before. I purchased my first Bible and began to study it. The *desire* for me to sin lessened dramatically with each passing day.

My vocabulary changed, the way I viewed myself changed, how I treated others changed, how I behaved with my boyfriend changed, etc. I was completely under construction. My heart began to feel conviction over the sensual way I was behaving with my boyfriend. Our love language at that time was physical touch.

The following week, my friend Valerie invited me to her church. We went that Sunday. When I arrived, there was a man in plain clothes speaking.

There was something in the atmosphere that was powerful, freeing, and pleasantly overwhelming. I gravitated to the way this man spoke; his enthusiasm was like a firework spectacular. He was so passionate about God. There was not a single dull moment. He encouraged everyone to open their Bibles and read along with him. The sermon was on the topic of sex. I was like a deer caught in headlights!! I thought that word was forbidden in church. Growing up, it certainly was a taboo subject. Quoting scripture, this man taught how sex is a beautiful gift from God for us to enjoy and cherish. Per God's design, the only prerequisite for sex is a marriage covenant.

He discussed how our bodies are temples of the Holy Spirit, and we are to honor God with our body and sexuality. It felt like God was speaking directly to me through this man.

The timing of this message and my attendance on that Sunday was no coincidence; it was a God instance. When I began a relationship with God, I obtained a new heart, a heart of obedience. I prayed for guidance, and God led me to this truth; when a man respects and loves a woman, he will wait with her.

I resolved to follow Christ, no matter what the cost. I was prepared to lose everything to pursue God.

Jesus was more than enough for me. I presented my conviction to my boyfriend, and thankfully, he had agreed to reset our relationship, honor God, and anchor ourselves in Christ. From that moment on, we began attending that Bible-teaching church together.

I passed my boards in July 2010, and on 1-1-11, Carlos asked me to be his wife.

In college, I began listening to podcast Christian ministries every night before bed. Daily messages that were twenty minutes in length and packed with encouragement.

I still had questions, and God led me to another

ministry, a place where I found evidence-based answers to life's difficult questions.

I began attending a weekly Bible study. My faith is just as exciting today as it was when the blinders were removed from my eyes. I had memorized the ten commandments at catechism as a young girl, and now, for the first time, I began to understand them.

My understanding began as I read NKJV Exodus 20:1-74 myself. It became clear how much God detests idols. God wants me to worship Him, the Creator, *not* the creation.

I reflected on how little I had communicated with God and how much time I spent bowing down to His creation. Though I feel utmost respect and admiration for the Disciples of Christ, the idols I associated with them served merely as a distraction.

I have been walking with Jesus for over a decade now, and each day he teaches me something new. Indeed, this is an exciting and fulfilling life.

Before my salvation, the attributes of God that were highlighted to me was the wrath of sin and consequent judgment. After my salvation, the attributes of God that are highlighted to me are God's love and subsequent mercy. The first part of my life was about observing. The second part is about experiencing. The first part was about memorizing. The second part is about understanding. The first part was about doing. The second part is about receiving what has already been done. The first part was all about me, and the second part is less of me and more of Him. The first part surrounded the question, what can I get out of God? In the second part, I am asking, what can't I give back to God?

My original works-based salvation theory dissolved very quickly. Now I understand that salvation comes by God's grace alone through faith in Christ. Good works come naturally as a byproduct of salvation. Our relationship with God always comes *before* obedience to Him. In the first nineteen years of my life I experienced religion, but in these last fourteen years I have experienced a relationship.

These are two totally different things. I think God is more interested in the condition of a person's heart than He is in rituals and repetitive motions, regardless of how respectful they may seem. God is interested and wants a relationship with each and every one of us. It is what He desires. God is chasing our hearts.

Allow me to ask, how can you explain the transformation of a person that did not own a Bible to now reading it daily? How can you explain a girl's bored obligation to go to church to now looking forward to and feeling blessed every time she goes? How do you explain the switch from only praying when she needs something from God to praying consistently because she simply wants to spend time with Him? How do you explain this fuel that keeps burning and only intensifies with time? This fire within that never burns out.

Regardless of the circumstances in life, how do you explain experiencing the loss of a child and only growing closer to God as a result? God is the only One that always, and completely, comforted me.

God understands our pain and can identify with it. God, the Father, suffered the temporary loss of his Son at Calvary. God's only Son, Jesus Christ, voluntarily took on the unimaginable suffering of dying on a cross for the payment of the world's sins. It was love that held Jesus there. Though God is not the author of pain, He certainly is not naïve to it. Suffering is not a foreign concept to God. It is in our pain and loneliness that God shows us His strength. There is absolutely no doubt that God's power is made *perfect* in our weakness.

I believe Jesus Christ is the Savior of the entire world. God's gift of salvation is available to everyone at any moment. Consider the criminal on the cross dying alongside Jesus. In his dying moment, he accepted Jesus... NKJV Luke 23:43 and Jesus said, "Assuredly, I say to you, today you will be with me in paradise." This is the God of the Bible that I follow. This is the Jesus that came to teach the high priest, the Pharisee, what it truly means to love his people. The sinner repented at his last breath. The intimate conversation took place between him and God; that man did not need a confessional; he did not need an intermediary. All he needed was God. It really is that simple.

The richest experience I have had with God took

place in my own home's privacy during my one-on-one devotion time with Him. God the Father wants everyone to come to the saving knowledge of His Son, Jesus Christ. God extends the invitation to everyone, and anyone can accept it.

Salvation is a gift from God, and it is yours for the taking. For years, God was chasing after my heart, and I was too distracted to pay attention.

I finally accepted the invitation, and I have been going from glory to glory ever since. I wholeheartedly agree with Apostle Paul's words in NKJV Philippians 1:21, "For to me, to live *is* Christ and to die *is* gain."

Monica Silva, Northern NJ

NKJV John 6: 38-40

38. "For I have come down from heaven, not to do my own will, but the will of Him who sent me. 39. This is the will of the Father who sent me, that all He has given me I should lose nothing but should raise it up and at the last day. 40. And this is the will of Him who sent Me, that everyone who sees the Son and believes in Him may have everlasting life; and I will raise him up at the last day."

NKJV Romans 5:8

"but God demonstrates His own love toward us, in that while we were still sinners, Christ died for us."

NKJV 1 John 1:9

"if we confess our sins, He is faithful and just to forgive us our sins and to cleanse us from all unrighteousness".

Ken's personal note: You will probably not remember all of your sins so you can finish with asking Him to forgive ALL of them and cleanse you from all unrighteousness. God knew all your transgressions even before you were born.

The Gospel (Good News)

You have read a book of stories. These stories are about a relationship with Jesus. Each person communicates how Jesus entered into the story of their lives.

These stories are all wrapped around a larger story - the story of God and His world. There are many ways to tell a story. I'd like to frame this story of good news of God and His world in a way that it has often been described, laying out the grand sweep of the world's history which has at its climax the death, burial, and resurrection of Jesus Christ. They are laid out almost like acts in the play: ***creation, fall, rescue, restoration, and response.***

CREATION

NKJV Psalm 90:2 - Before the mountains were brought forth, or ever you had formed the earth in the world, even from everlasting to everlasting, you are God.

NKJV Genesis 1:1 - In the beginning God created the heavens and the earth.

NKJV Genesis 1:31 – Then God saw everything that he had made, and indeed it was very good. So the evening and the morning were the sixth day.

You are the product of God's creative efforts. The very existence of a complex being, the human, is a proof that a more complex being brought him or her into existence. Yes, this still involves a measure of faith, but it is not an unreasonable faith if you look around you and ponder how our complex world came into being.

The Bible teaches that God brought into existence a world characterized by peace and goodness. God created, and that was good. Artists create because they were made in the image of God, but everything they bring into existence is made out of something in the already existing world, which was brought into being out of nothing by the creator extraordinaire. When you grasp how excellent God is, you begin to realize just how inferior we are.

We are the masters of our creations, not the other way around. Technology is a great example of this. We create technology to serve our efforts on this earth. Should it surprise us then that God is the Master of His creation? Should we then serve ourselves or the one who made us? God created us for a loving relationship with Him and then brings Him the greatest glory and joy. Sadly, without exception, all of humanity has rejected God's love toward them.

FALL

NKJV Genesis 2:16-17 16. And the Lord God commanded the man, saying, "Of every tree of the garden you may freely eat; 17. but of the tree of the knowledge of good and evil you shall not eat, for in the day that you eat of it you shall surely die."

NKJV Genesis 3:6 - So when the woman saw that the tree was good for food, that it was pleasant to the eyes, and that the tree desirable to make one wise, she took of its fruit and ate. She also gave to her husband with her, and he ate.

NKJV Romans 3:23 - for all have sinned and fall short of the glory of God,

NKJV Romans 6:23 - For the wages of sin is death, but the gift of God is eternal life in Christ Jesus our Lord.

The first humans, Adam and Eve, were given instructions and boundaries. Do I know why God established these boundaries? At the end of the day and with my limited knowledge, I quite frankly do not know. However, I do know the Creator God as being loving and good towards His creation, so I can conjecture that God established them for safety and security of relationship, but also for choice in relationship. God loved the humans He created, but He was not going to force them into loving Him back.

They chose sin - the outright rejection of God's

authority and the callous disobedience of God's instructions. This is rebellion to its very core. These actions spurned the one who created them, provided for them, and love them.

Lest you think that you are holier than Adam and Eve, God's Word puts you in the same category that they are in - rebellious sinner. Yes, all of humanity is in that category, both actively and passively.

You see, everyone actively makes choices that go against God's instructions. Not only that, but at the beginning of the book of Romans in the Bible a picture is painted of a person who is in a broken relationship with God because they passively did not glorify God or show their gratitude to Him.

We would all speak out against an individual who was ungrateful towards another person who saved their life. Yet, God gave all the people life and so many continue going their way without acknowledging God's existence or being grateful to Him. No wonder their relationship with God is broken.

There is a break in every human's relationship with God in desperate need of repair. If left to people, it will not and cannot be fixed. God, though, in His great kindness provided a way for the relationship to be made right. He did so through a twist in the story that no-one saw coming. God became a man who lived perfectly as the God-man and both provided the payment of what was owed due to man's rebellion and paved a way back to God.

His name is Jesus, and He is your rescuer.

RESCUE

NKJV Genesis 3:15 – And I will put enmity between you and the woman, and between your seed and her Seed; He shall bruise your head, and you shall bruise His heel."

NKJV 1 Peter 3:18 - for Christ also suffered once for sins, the just for the unjust, that He might bring us to God, being put to death in the flesh but made alive by the spirit,

NKJV Galatians 1:3-5 3. Grace to you and peace from God the Father and our Lord Jesus Christ, 4. who gave Himself for our sins, that He might deliver us from this present evil age, according to the will of our God and Father, 5. to whom be glory forever and ever. Amen.

NKJV Romans 3:23-24 – 23. for all have sinned and fall short of the glory of God, 24. Being justified freely by His grace through the redemption that is in Christ Jesus,

NKJV Romans 6:23 - for the wages of sin is death, but the gift of God is eternal life in Christ Jesus our Lord.

God had made the promise of a rescuer way back in history after Adam and Eve led the first rebellion against God. He promised that a deliverer would come and suffer for those who had done evil even though He never had.

Jesus is part of the Trinity - a man-made term for a reality found in the Bible that God is three persons yet one God. God the Father, Jesus, and the Holy Spirit are all fully God yet exist as three persons. Yes, it is hard to comprehend, and we will never fully understand it, but since when can a created thing fully know the one who created?

Jesus came to earth, conceived in Virgin Mary's womb. He was born a perfect child untainted by any sin. He also lived a perfect life and complete adherence to all instructions given by God the Father, so that he could be the perfect sacrifice for the sins of all those who would trust in his work. It was proven that he was the perfect sacrifice by His resurrection from the dead. You can see threads of this plan all throughout the Bible, being spoken about for thousands of years and culminated when Jesus endured Roman capital punishment on a cross while being truly perfect and guiltless. The innocent was punished so that the guilty could live. You are guilty, but Jesus is your rescuer.

You do play a part in this rescue. Your role is your own repentance and faith. You repent of your rebellion towards God, embracing Jesus' payment on the cross for your sin, depending on Jesus' work for you to have a right relationship with God, having faith by trusting in Jesus.

God is not only the rescuer, He is also the restorer.

RESTORATION

NKJV Revelation 21:4 – And God will wipe away every tear from their eyes; shall be no more death, nor sorrow, nor crying. There shall be no more pain, for the former things have passed away."

NKJV Revelation 22:3-5 – 3. And there shall be no more curse, but the throne of God and of the Lamb shall be in it, and His servants shall serve Him. 4. They shall see His face, and His name shall be on their foreheads. 5. There shall be no more night there: They need no lamp nor light of the sun, for the Lord God gives them light. And they shall reign forever and ever.

What will it be like when the restoration process is complete the Creator God is about His plan not only to rescue and redeem his creation but also to restore a beautiful and full relationship between Creator and creation. The relationship will be whole and close at last.

God will one day make all things new again and be in an eternal and perfect relationship with His people. Pieces of it are described in the Bible, but the description will not do it justice. When we experience what this heaven is like, we will find that we never had the capacity of words to describe its beauty and wonder, for it will far exceed any expectations we had. Imagine that. Heaven and an eternal relationship with God will suppress all the hype and expectations we had in our minds!

Response

How will you respond to these stories and this story of God and humans? This story is not a good work of fiction that leaves you with emotional feelings at the end. This story is reality and it must be responded to. Let me propose a course of action.

1. **Admit your need**. We do not like to believe that we need anything. We are brought up to be self-sufficient beings who work hard at providing for our needs. In order to be set right with God, you must come to the realization that there is absolutely no action that you can take to make things right again. You must recognize that you are in need of God's actions on your behalf to be set right with Him.

2. **Ask Him to forgive you.** You rebelled against your creator, both actively and passively, by disobeying His instructions and not bringing Him glory and thanks with your life. Talk to Him. He will listen. Pour out your heart. He will forgive you. Just ask.

3. **Trust in Jesus alone to rescue you.** We do not like admitting our need, and we do not like needing a rescuer. Have faith in Jesus. He has done what is needed to rescue you.

4. **Follow Jesus Christ.** Learn what it means to be a follower of Jesus. Get involved with a church family who encourage one another in following Jesus and who gather together regularly to be taught the Word of God. Do not stop there in your learning, though, become a student of the Bible yourself.

5. **Learn Jesus' teachings.** The CSB (Christian Standard Bible), ESV (English Standard Version), the NLT (New Living Translation), the NKJV (New Kings James Version) and NIV (New International Version) are great translations of the Bible to explore and learn from.

6. **Tell your story.** You read a book of stories. You learned about the story of the world. Now share your story with others. There is no greater relationship that anyone can have in their lifetime than a relationship with their Creator. You can be the conduit to the restoration of someone else with God, Our Creator and Savior.

Pastor Rick Dobrowolski, Allentown Bible Church, located in Allentown, PA

Final thoughts

Point of information about the Bible. There are many versions such as English Standard Version (ESV), New International Version (NIV), King James Version (KJV), to name a few. I have used the New King James Version (NKJV) for this book. Some will have study Bibles with a chapter explanation on each page side, which I still find helpful.

The Bible is God's **Word** showing his love for all humanity. The Bible begins with Genesis, the creation of the world. This is the first book of the Old Testament, which contains a total of 39 books. The New Testament consists of 27 books, starting with the introduction of Jesus Christ and John the Baptist. The Bible concludes with the book of Revelation.

As a new reader of the Bible, it is usually suggested to start with the book of John and then Romans.

The people who have accepted and surrendered entirely to Jesus Christ are known as Christians, born-again, believers or followers of Jesus Christ. Your relationship with God is what is essential for you in this life and more importantly, for eternity.

Ken Byrne